Hitler's Olympics - The Facts

John R Webb

Hitler's Olympics - The Facts

John R Webb

Copyright © 2019 Sanctuary Press Ltd

ISBN-13: 978-1-913176-09-9

Sanctuary Press Ltd
71-75 Shelton Street
Covent Garden
London
WC2H 9JQ

www.sanctuarypress.com
Email: info@sanctuarypress.com

"Sporting and chivalrous competition awakens the best human qualities. It does not sever, but on the contrary, unites the opponents in mutual understanding and reciprocal respect. It also helps to strengthen the bonds of peace between the nations. May the Olympic Flame therefore never be extinguished." - Adolf Hitler [1]

1. Quoted in *The XIth Olympic Games Berlin, 1936,* Official Report, Volume I, Organisation Committee for the XIth Olympiad Berlin 1936, page 6

View of the Olympic thoroughfare, Unter den Linden, from the top of the Brandenburg Gate.

The official Olympic poster. Design: Werner Würbel, Berlin.

Adolf Hitler with the Reich Minister of the Interior, Dr. Frick, on the site of the Reich Sport Field on October 5th, 1933.

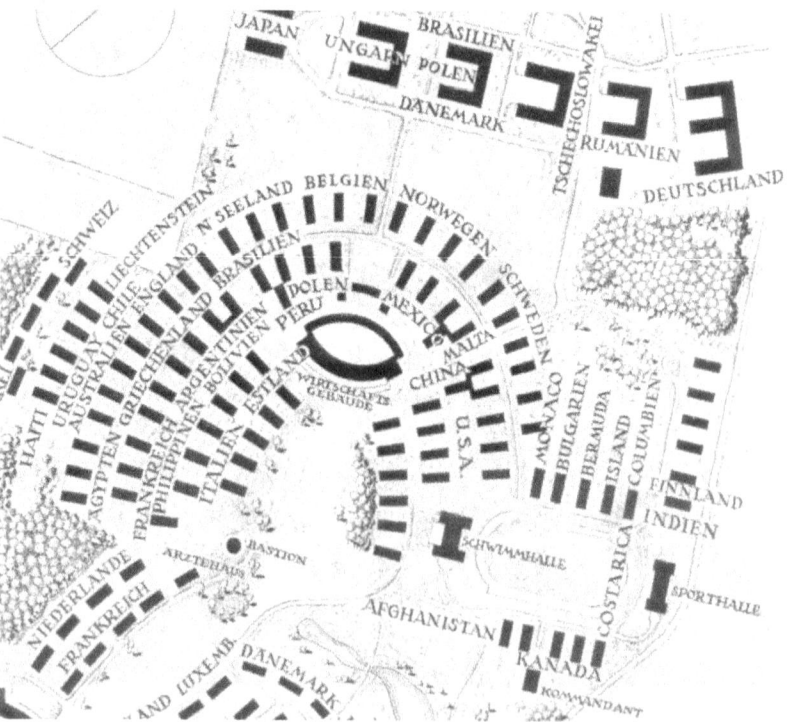

Plan for athlete accommodation blocks.

THE OLYMPICS COME TO GERMANY

It was a highly confident and successful Germany that hosted the 1936 Olympics in Berlin. In three years the 'Nazi economic miracle' had eliminated mass unemployment completely in a country that had no gold reserves, no empire and no friends. On the other hand, the 'democracies', with their gold, empires and 'market forces', were still languishing in depression and decay.

Arriving for the Games athletes and spectators found swastikas everywhere, including 45-foot high banners in Berlin's main avenue. It is said that all signs of anti-Semitism and concentration camps were removed, as were notices and graffiti abusing Jews. Works of writers banned since 1933 reappeared in bookshops.[2] It may be noted that there was no such reprieve for books banned by the 'democratic' government of West Germany when it hosted the 1972 Olympics.

One sports historian opposed to the Nazis, George Eisen, has written that[3] *"owners of several large Jewish stores in Berlin, who otherwise were prohibited from exhibiting the German flag and emblem, were instructed by the propaganda ministry to participate in the ordered general display of flags."* Incidentally, therefore, he confirms that in 1936 there were still "several large Jewish stores in Berlin."

---

2 Peter Padfield, *Flight for the Fuhrer*, Weidenfeld and Nicolson, London, page 87. In this context, the expression "anti-Semitism" refers to anti-Jewish sentiment, which unfortunately existed in Germany as in many other countries at the time. Arabs are also Semites, but they did not attract such negativism.

3 George Eisen, "The Voices of Sanity: American Diplomatic Reports from the 1936 Berlin Olympiad," *Journal of Sports History*, Vol. 11, No 3 (Winter, 1984), page 74. Mr Eisen is cited as an Associate Professor of Health, Physical Education, Recreation and Dance at the California State Polytechnic. It is interesting to note that, in June 1933, shortly after coming to power, Hitler actually authorised the investment of 14.5 million Reich Marks in the Jewish Hertie department store chain to save it from collapse (David Schoenbaum, *Hitler's Social Revolution*, Wiedenfeld & Nicolson 1967, page 141).

The Olympic structures, close to the edge of the city.

THE BOYCOTT CAMPAIGN

The decision to hold the 1936 Games in Germany was taken in 1931, the Germans easily overcoming their main rival Spain, which wanted the Games to be held in Barcelona, despite the political turmoil in Spain at the time. However, following the formation of Hitler's government in 1933, an international campaign was let loose to choose a new venue or get sportsmen to boycott the event. This was in spite of the obvious need to promote international friendship and understanding at the time. The protagonists for the boycott argued, ultimately unsuccessfully, that Germany, by its attitude to Jewish athletes, had violated the Olympic rules, which forbid discrimination. Jews could not compete on an equal footing, it was said, as they had separate clubs and were denied adequate opportunities for training and competition.[4]

---

4 "Olympic Games in Germany, Case Against Taking Part", *The Manchester Guardian,* 5 December 1935.

The May Field with the Bell Tower above the speaker's stand.

US DIPLOMATS MISCHIEF-MAKING

Disgracefully, in contrast to the attitude of the British and French envoys to Germany, the three leading American diplomats in Germany lent their powerful support to the boycott campaign: William E Dodd (Ambassador), George S Messerssmith (Consul General) and Raymond H Geist (Consul). They were *"perceived by their superiors as men of principle ... [who] often went beyond diplomatic niceties,"* and they were *"unanimously vocal in their belief that the holding of the festival on German soil would constitute a disaster for the free-world."* [5]

The outcome showed, perhaps, why they thought it would be a 'disaster'. Even the anti-Nazi journalist William Shirer, author of *The Rise and Fall of the Third Reich*, who was working in Germany during this period, had to admit that [6] *"... the visitors,*

5   Eisen, page 57

6   William I Shirer, *Rise and Fall of the Third Reich*, New York 1960, page 233, as quoted by Eisen.

especially those from England and America, were greatly impressed by what they saw ... a far different picture, they said, than they got from reading newspaper dispatches from Berlin." Presumably Dodd & Co did not want people to see the real National Socialist Germany for themselves.

SOVIET SUPPORT FOR THE BOYCOTT

The communist authorities in Moscow supported Dodd and his fellow diplomatic representatives of capitalism. *The Times* of London reported in 1935:[7]

"The Comintern (Third International), which held its 'world congress' in Moscow in August, has since taken what is described several 'momentous decisions' involving 'radical changes' in its tactics abroad..." One of the 'momentous decisions' was to reorganise its international youth movement in order to *"... entice children and adolescents of existing [non-communist] organisations into becoming members..."*

Only Fascism was to be attacked (not capitalism) and a firm footing had to be gained in all spheres of activity, "*especially in sport,*" and the report continued: *"One of the immediate tasks is to defeat the plans for holding the next Olympic Games in Germany.*" The Soviet Union itself boycotted the Games, as it had on previous occasions, and so did the Popular Front government of Spain – exposing its true nature before the outbreak of the Spanish Civil War. [8]

---

7   "Moscow's New Campaign: Intrigue Among Youth," The Times, London, 21 November 1935.

8   The Popular Front government in Spain tried, unsuccessfully, to organise an alternative spoiler Games proclaimed as 'The People's Olympiad'. The event was due to be held in Barcelona (which had been rejected as the Olympic venue in 1931 by the International Olympic Committee) and commence in the middle of July 1936, two weeks before the proper Olympics. However, the whole event was aborted when the Spanish Civil War broke out one day before it was due to start.

8

The May Field during the gymnastic demonstration of the young people at the Olympic Games.

OLYMPIC COMMITTEE INVESTIGATES

As early as June 1933 the International Olympic Committee asked Germany for reassurances on the conduct of the Games and the German government guaranteed, *"as a principle German Jews should not be excluded from German teams."* [9] Agitation continued and further assurances were given. In fact, the president of the German organising committee, Dr Lewald, a member of the International Committee, was himself a grandson of a Jew. The American Consul General Messersmith, however, warned the US State Department that Dr Lewald, a respected figure in the International Olympics scene for decades, could not be trusted.[10]

It is true that there was discrimination against Jews in many sports in Germany, but this was not due to any legislation or official demands. Indeed, the Reichskomissar for Sport, von Tschammer und Osten, issued an instruction to all sport associations in Germany, *"giving them a free hand to decide for themselves*

9 "Olympic Games in Germany, Case Against Taking Part", *The Manchester Guardian*, 5 December 1935.

10 Eisen, page 63

The Dietrich Eckart Open-Air Theatre.

whether or not to exclude non-Aryans from membership. "[11] The Hitler government evidently felt that private individuals and clubs should be free to choose whom they associated with. This is in stark contrast, of course, to the practice in many self-styled democratic countries today, where compulsory multi-culturalism is enforced through the use of draconian laws.

The discrimination against Jews was unfortunate and seems particularly unwholesome today, but it reflected the great tension between Germans and Jews at the time. It should be remembered also that discrimination against Jews was evident in other countries as well. Indeed, one highly reputable left-wing historian has pointed out that [12] *"... Jews were treated as badly in other countries, and often worse – Poland, for example, with whom, nevertheless, Great Britain remained on friendly terms."*

Complaints about the exclusion of Jews from golf clubs in Britain were still being made long after the end of WW2.[13]

---

11 *Eisen*, page 58, quoting from a report to the US Secretary of State by Consul Raymond Geist dated 13 December 1933.

12 AJP Taylor, *English History, 1914–1945*, Oxford University Press 1976, page 419.

13 For example, *The Times*, London, reported on 29 February 1960, "Golf Clubs

JEWISH PARTICIPATION

German Jews, indeed, had two sports organisations of their own – the Maccabi and the Schild (the sports branch of the Jewish ex-soldiers association) – that were free to run their own events. 21 athletes from these two organisations accepted invitations to take part in Olympic training camps during 1934-36, but no-one amongst them was good enough to be selected for the final team.

In fact, two Jewish athletes, Helene Mayer and Gretel Bergman, returned to Germany to compete in the 1936 Games *at the invitation of the German Government.* Also, the ice hockey player Rudi Ball, who had been living in France, played for Germany in the Winter Olympics held in Bavaria. Mayer had won a gold medal in the 1928 Olympics and come fifth in the event at the Los Angeles Games in 1932, after which she decided to stay on to study at the University of Southern California - before Hitler came to power. She clearly recovered her form as she won the US women's fencing championships in 1934 and 1935.

There was no restriction on other countries including Jews in their teams. Indeed, there seem to have no restrictions at all on foreign visitors or officials, even from hostile countries. It is a fact that 13 Jews were medal winners at the Games – just one less than the total medal winners for Great Britain (which had no Jews among its own medal winners). Among those 13 were eight gold medal winners – twice as many as Great Britain could muster. The fair and proper conduct of the Berlin Games may be compared with the spiteful exclusion from Britain of the head of the Syrian National Olympic Committee in 2012;[14] the barring from the London Games of the brilliant Greek athlete Voula Papachristou for posting an allegedly 'racist' joke on the internet

---

Deny Ban on Jews," after the Bishop of Southwark quoted allegations against several clubs. According to *The Times*, the secretary of one of these clubs said: "We have one or two Jewish members. There is no ban on them. But the main feeling in this club is that they have their own clubs and that they would probably prefer to go to those clubs."

14 "Syrian Olympic chief banned from London 2012," *Guardian*, London, 22 June 2012.

and expressing support for a legal 'far right' political party; [15] the expulsion from the same Games of the Swiss footballer Michel Morganella, again for posting an allegedly 'racist' comment on the internet; [16] and the disgraceful treatment of the German rower Nadja Drygalla, who left the London Olympic village in 2012 *"of her own accord after a 90-minute conversation with German officials,"* because her boyfriend was 'exposed' as a member of the National Democratic Party – a legal political party with elected representatives in two German States. [17]

FACT-FINDING MISSIONS

In view of the international agitation against the Games, Avery Brundage, the president of the American Olympic Association, was sent on a fact-finding tour of Germany in 1934, possibly as a consequence of Messersmith's intervention. Charles E Sherrill, a member of both the American and International Olympic Committees, undertook a further trip in 1935. Both of these officials, presumably trusted and respected by their organisations, were satisfied with the arrangements for the Games. However, these missions are said to have exemplified everything that Messersmith loathed." [18]

Perhaps Messersmith loathed the idea of people going to Germany to get facts at first hand for themselves, rather than relying on what was said by those who were admittedly prejudiced against the new Germany. It seems unlikely that two such respected figures in the Olympic movement would not undertake their missions honestly. It may be noted that the great Jesse Owens, on his return to America after the Games, referred specifically to Avery Brundage as a "fine Man." [19]

15 "Kicked out for a racist tweet: Greek triple jumper is banned from the Games after her African 'joke'," *Daily Mail*, London, 25 July 2012.

16 "Footballer Michel Morganella expelled from Games for allegedly racist tweet," *Daily Telegraph*, London, 30 July 2012.

17 "German rower leaves Olympics over 'Nazi boyfriend' allegations," *Guardian*, London, 3 August 2012.

18 Eisen, page 66.

19 "Owens arrives with kind words for all officials," United Press agency report, *The Pittsburg Press*, 24 August 1936.

US Ambassador William E Dodd

DODD COMES TO GRIEF

It seems that Dodd did all he could to sabotage the Games. When Dr Lewald tried to approach the US Embassy in Berlin, Dodd,[20] *"who made no effort to hide his contempt for National Socialism, rather amusedly cabled these overtures to Cordell Hull [US Secretary of State]."*

Even though he was the US Ambassador, he refused to meet Dr Lewald, who was anxious to explain and justify the German position. Instead, he contemptuously sent a low level embassy official to meet Dr Lewald to have just an informal discussion.[21]

Dodd was removed from his post in 1937 and, in the following year, he knocked down a 4 year old African-American child in his car and fled the scene of the accident. The child sustained severe injuries but Dodd did not stop to help; he was subsequently apprehended and got away with a fine of about £60.[22] So much for this 'man of principle'.

---

20 Eisen, page 70.

21 *Ibid.*

22 "William Dodd (ambassador)," Wikipedia, accessed 19 July 2012.

ABSURD ALLEGATIONS

As they could not rely on facts to support their case, the opponents of the Berlin Games ascribed the most absurd ulterior motives to the Germans. Thus Consul Geist, as early as at the end of 1933, reported that [23] *"All forms of physical culture and sport will be made a part of the general political scheme of the Hitler Government. Sport will make him [the German] physically fit to endure the hardships of military life."*

The same comment could, perhaps, be made about other countries, particularly Britain which, at the time of the 2012 Olympics, had been almost continually engaged in wars and other military operations on three continents for the previous 20 years. It may be noted, of course, that Hitler's Government also encouraged women to take part in physical activity and sport and they did not have to endure the hardships of military life – unlike women in Britain's armed forces today. [24] Geist, in his 1933 report, also seemed to find something sinister in the facilities to be provided for the Berlin Games, stating that, for Hitler [25] *"even the enlarged stadium was too small, the German sport idea must be represented by something truly colossal, the whole district surrounding the stadium and the university for physical culture must be transformed into one gigantic athletic plant."*

The same could probably said of every country that hosts the Games. It certainly seems to apply to Britain, which had a budget (according to official figures) of £9.3 billion for preparations for the 2012 Games. These preparations included the demolition of a 2.5 square kilometre area of East London and, among other things, this work apparently required the removal of no less than 52 electricity pylons with power lines being transferred into two giant 6km-long tunnels. [26]

---

23 Eisen, page 65.

24 In 2012, the year of Britain's Olympics, it was reported that a pregnant woman soldier gave birth on Britain's front line in Afghanistan ["MoD rule out pregnancy tests for frontline women," *Daily Mail*, London, 19 September 2012].

25 Eisen, page 66.

26 "Preparation works Building London 2012 Olympics," Official London 2012

THE 'TOKENISM' ALLEGATION

Geist, in his report of December 1933 warned *"it does not seem likely that they [Jewish athletes] can represent Germany in international competition."* Nevertheless, he came forward with the alternative scenario of 'tokenism' lest his prediction might come crushing down in the reality of facts. He asserted [27] *"It may, however, be that in view of foreign pressure and the outlook of losing the money and prestige which the Olympic Games will bring to Germany, the German sport authorities will drop certain restrictive measures taken against Jews. But it appears unlikely that this will be anything but a meaningless gesture."*

This opinion was echoed by Messersmith's comment (described by Eisen as '*a most astute observation on German intentions*'): [28] *"It is not impossible that in order to put up a screen a few Jews may be allowed to train and to figure on teams; but I think it should be understood that this will be merely a screen for the real discrimination which is taking place."*

This argument falls apart as, in 1935 – before the boycott campaign had been defeated – the German Government passed the so-called Nuremberg Race Laws, which introduced new restrictions on the Jews. These laws removed Jewish entitlement to German citizenship, banned the intermarriage of Jews and Aryans and prohibited the employment by Jews of female Aryan servants under the age of 35. So, far from dropping restrictive measures prior to the Games, the German Government introduced new ones. If the Germans were going to make concessions for the sake of the Olympics, surely they would have put the Nuremberg Laws on the back burner until after the Games.

---

website [www.london2012.com – accessed 20 October 2012].

27 Eisen, page 66.

28 Eisen, page 61.

Adolf Hitler Platz leading to the Olympic Stadium.

DRAGGING POLITICS INTO SPORT

Count Baillet Latour, the president of the International Olympic Committee, referred to attempts to deprive Germany of the Olympics as *'political machinations'*. He pointed out that, had the opposition arisen among athletes, the leaders of sport in their countries would have been compelled to support the boycott. However, on the contrary [29] *"... they had energetically resisted all such machinations which were clearly an attempt to draw sport into the service of politics."* Count Baillet's exposure of the boycott campaign did not deter those who were behind the machinations. If anything, it spurred them to greater efforts, fortunately all in vain.

---

29 "Next Olympic Games," *The Times*, London, 7 November 1935.

Water is let into the diving pool of the Swimming Stadium for the first time.

BOYCOTT CAMPAIGN DEFEATED

A month before a crucial decision on the matter by the American Athletic Union, US Consul General Messersmith issued a final sanctimonious warning that [30] *"unless the American [Olympic] Committee can definitely satisfy itself by first-hand knowledge and observation that this discrimination no longer takes place, I do not believe that it would remain a representative of American sport tradition if American athletes participate in the Olympic Games in 1936."* This was at a time when racial segregation in the United States was at its height.

---

30 Eisen, page 65.

The Italian team marching past the War Memorial on Unter den Linden.

Despite immense pressure from international trouble-makers, the anti-German campaign was finally defeated in December 1935 when the national Convention of the American Athletic Union, the largest organisation of its kind in America, decided, by 61 votes to 55, not to withdraw its members from the Games. The union itself later ratified the decision. This stand may well have

The Olympic competitors from every nation honoured the soldiers who fell in the Great War.

been very influential in determining the position of other national Olympic organisations. The failure of the boycott campaign was underlined by the participation of a record number of entries. Forty-nine nations took part, twelve more than at the previous Games in 1932 at Los Angeles. Even its detractors had to admit that the Berlin Games were a stunning success.

The Olympic torch is lit at the beginning of a 1,100 kilometre journey to Berlin.

THE TORCH RELAY

One of the most outstanding innovations at the Berlin Games was the torch relay – a spectacular and moving pageant that has become a standard feature of the Olympics ever since. As the ancient Games were designed to promote peace and harmony among competing States, so the Germans wished to encourage the same spirit in keeping with their government's policy. Hitler, whose peace and disarmament initiatives had generally been ignored, had demonstrated his sincerity in the Anglo-German Naval Agreement 1935; aware of British concern about the

The Olympic torch arrives at the stadium.

growing German Navy prior to the First World War, he agreed to limit the new German Navy to just 35% the size of the British. The torch ceremonies symbolised this spirit.

20th July 1936 was declared a public holiday in Greece and young and old turned out to celebrate the start of the Olympics, At dawn, in the shadow of Mount Olympus, the first runner took the lighted torch on a relay that was to traverse seven countries over 1,100 kilometres. A hymn was chanted and musicians played ancient instruments. At each town on the way to the Bulgarian frontier there were ceremonies to bless the torch as it passed through. Over 3,000 runners carried the torch to Berlin, all the way on foot. There were no rides on metros, rowing boats, funfairs or other gimmicks as evident in the London Games of 2012, where the torch was seen accompanied by buses advertising Coca Cola, Lloyds Bank and other commercial sponsors, overwhelming the original Olympic spirit.

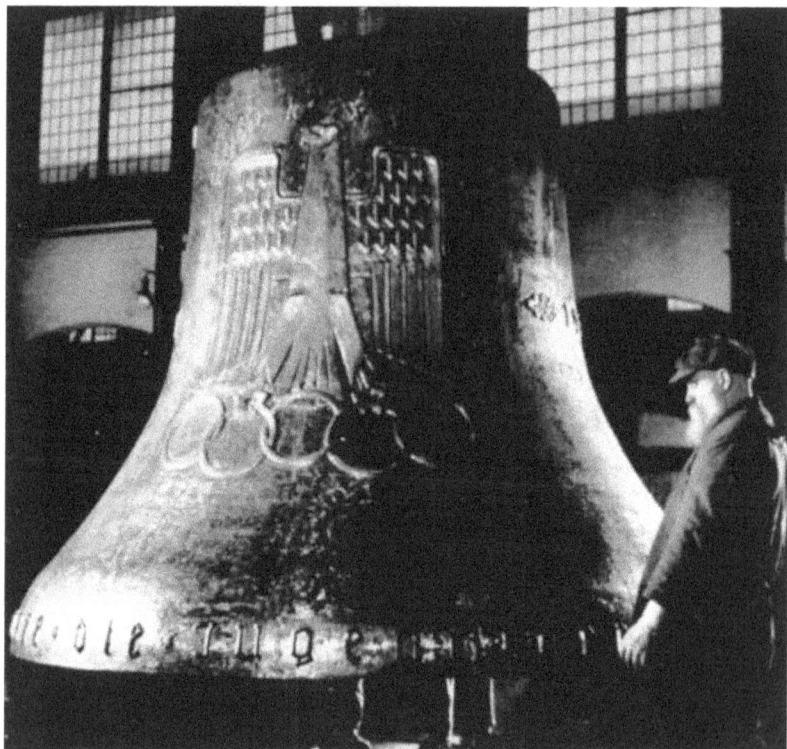

Cooling, polishing, chasing and tuning—and the Olympic Bell is completed.

THE OLYMPIC BELL

Another innovation for the Berlin Games was the Olympic Bell, the ringing of which marked the opening of the Games. Designed by the sculptor Walter E Lemcke, it was made at the oldest cast steel bell factory in the world in the Rhineland. The bell weighed over nine tons and was over nine foot in diameter and nearly nine foot in height. It was beautifully embossed with representations of: the Brandenburg Gate; the German Eagle holding the Olympic rings in its talons; two discreet swastikas; and the inspiring slogan, "I summon the youth of the world," taken from one of Schiller's famous poems.

Its journey from the Rhineland to Berlin was a triumphal procession that was greeted all along its route by local people, factory sirens and the peeling of church bells; and it was escorted by a

22

The bell is moved from the Rhineland foundry to the Olympic stadium.

host of different organisations. It was installed in a bell tower over 250 feet high, from the top of which the whole of Berlin could be seen. The importance of this new and enduring symbol to the Olympic Organising Committee is evidenced by the fact that nine pages of their official report are dedicated to it. [31]

Miraculously, the Olympic Stadium emerged from the Second World War virtually unscathed. However, during the war the tower was used to store film archives and these were set on fire by Soviet troops, using the tower as a chimney. The British Army of Occupation then took over the Stadium as its headquarters and, in 1947 - two years after the end of the war - they destroyed the tower. The bell, not being removed beforehand, crashed to the ground. The resulting long crack can still be seen and has prevented the bell from sounding ever since. In 1962, perhaps because they belatedly realised that a German army was necessary to protect Europe from the Soviet hordes, the British faithfully restored the tower in accordance with the original plans, engaging the original architect for the purpose. The tower is now an important tourist destination. All the original embossing can still be seen, but the two swastikas are now only partially visible, presumably as a result of vandalism.

31 Official Report, pages 111-119.

THE OPENING CEREMONY

At the opening ceremony of the Olympics[32] " ... *a crowd of 110,000 cheered as Hitler took his place on the official stand. Some of the delegations used the Olympic salutation, a stiff right arm extended to the side but, to the delight of the audience, Austrians modified this to the Nazi salute ... The greatest applause came for the 250-member French team whose salute was more Roman than Olympian. ... The Americans team got the least applause, and some stamping of feet, as they passed the Tribute of Honour, eyes right, without dipping their flags.*"

The American action was, perhaps, to be expected. At the 1908 Olympics in London, the US contingent was the only one not to dip its colours in salute to King Edward VII's royal box during the parade of athletes.[33] Nevertheless, the German crowds in Berlin were wildly enthusiastic and appreciative of all competitors at the Games, including the Americans, black and white.

---

32 John Toland, *Adolf Hitler*, Doubleday & Co, New York 1976, page 392.

33 *The Barnes Review*, Washington, August 1996.

THE 'OLYMPIAN' SALUTE

One of the most spectacular scenes at the Olympics was the sight of over 100.000 people (many of whom must have been foreigners) rising and giving the famous right arm salute at significant moments in the Games. The salute goes by various names today: 'Roman', 'Fascist', 'Nazi', and 'Hitler'. But it was sometimes difficult to distinguish it from the 'Olympian' salute, which was almost identical. In fact the Olympian salute seems to have had the same symbolism for Olympians as the Roman did for Fascists. For they both seem to derive from a timeless tradition where the person who raises his right arm is demonstrating that he is not intending or, indeed, able to draw his sword from its hilt, whilst the open hand shows sincerity and friendship. This salute may be compared with the one adopted by communists and other left-wing elements – the clenched fist salute of hatred and aggression. The Black Power salute, famously demonstrated at the 1968 Olympics, appears to be a rather confused combination of both, with the raised right arm but a clenched fist.

The Canadian team at the 1936 Winter Olympics giving the "Olympic" salute.

At the Winter Olympics in Bavaria held earlier in 1936, most teams gave a right arm salute (with open hand), which German broadcasters described as a 'German' salute. This seems to have embarrassed the Austrian contingent (Austria had a totalitarian and strongly anti-Nazi government at the time) and its representative was quick to assert that they had given the 'Olympian' salute.[34] As mentioned above, at the Summer Games their intention seems to have been somewhat clearer. In any event, it is not easy to discern much difference in the salutes; their similarity is so close that the 'Olympian' has been effectively banned as a result of political correctness and, in some countries, by law.

---

34 "The Olympic Salute," *The Times*, London, 11 February 1936.

THE RELAY CONTROVERSY

It is said sometimes that, towards the end of the athletics, the Americans dropped two Jewish sprinters from their 4 x 100 metres relay team on Nazi insistence. Apparently, so it has been alleged, the Nazis did not want to be humiliated by Jews beating them as well as African-Americans.[35]

The affair was described in Jesse's obituary in the *New York Times* in the following terms:[36] *"Actually, Mr. Owens had not been scheduled to run in the relay. Marty Glickman and Sam Stoller were, but American Olympic officials, led by Avery Brundage, wanted to avoid offending the Nazis. They replaced Mr. Glickman and Mr. Stoller, both Jews, with Mr. Owens and Ralph Metcalfe, both blacks."*

The facts however, were plainly stated by the sports correspondent of a leading liberal newspaper in Britain, who was reporting from the Games *at the time they were actually taking place.* He wrote: [37] *"Mr Lawson Robertson, the chief American coach, has decided to run Owens in the 4 x 100 meters relay after all, as the Germans have done an exceptionally fast trial during the past few days, and the Americans are not absolutely confident of victory."*

As Jesse Owens and Ralph Metcalfe (who had come second in the 100 metres final) had given outstanding performances in the earlier races, it seems perfectly reasonable that they should be extended to run another race in order to meet an apparently unexpected threat from the German relay athletes. Of course, if Hitler and the Nazis had been so enraged and humiliated by Owens's success in earlier races, it would seem a strange way to "avoid offending" them by entering him in yet another race.

---

35 Philip Delves Broughton, "Forget Hitler – it was America that snubbed Jesse Owens," *Daily Mail*, London, 12 August 2009.

36 "Jesse Owens dies of cancer at 66; Hero of the 1936 Berlin Olympics," Frank Litsky, *New York Times*, 1 April 1980.

37 R.A. Hewins, "Lessons of the Olympiad," *The Observer*, 9 August 1936.

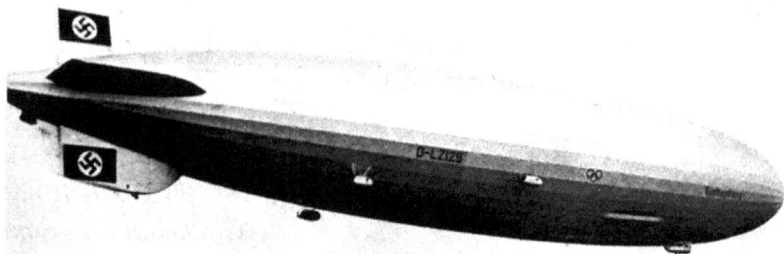

The Hindenburg airship passes over the Olympic stadium.

In any event, as previously mentioned, no fewer than 13 Jews won medals at the Games. As well as Helene Mayer, these included Samuel Balter who won a gold medal as part of the American basketball team.

THE PERUVIAN FOOTBALL DISPUTE

A dispute arose between Peru and Austria (then an independent country) about their quarter final match in the football competition, but it provided another opportunity to have a go at Hitler. As stated in Wikipedia,[38] *"Hitler called for a rematch of the quarter finals match to discount Peru's 4–2 win over Austria. The Peruvian national Olympic team refused to play the match again and withdrew from the games."*

The British popular daily newspaper *The Mirror* also reported, when excitement for the 2012 Games was reaching a peak, that Hitler had called for a rematch, referring to the episode as one of "100 bizarre facts about the Olympics." [39]

Contemporary accounts however provide a different interpretation. At the time of the affair, a popular British newspaper the *Daily Sketch* reported that about 1,000 Peruvian supporters stormed on to the pitch with "iron bars, knives and even

---

38 "Racism in Sport," Wikipedia. [accessed 25 October 2012.]

39 Steve Anglesey, "Weird of the Rings: 100 Bizarre facts about the Olympic Games," *Mirror*, 16 July 2012.

a pistol." [40] *The Times* reported that the game had been a very rough one, *"with the Peruvians apparently more at fault than their opponents."* Tempers flared on and off the pitch, with some Peruvian fans invading the pitch and kicking an Austrian player. The Austrians protested to FIFA, the governing body for international football, which decided that the match should be replayed with no spectators admitted. The Peruvians did not turn up for the replay, the Austrians were given a walkover and the Peruvians then announced their withdrawal from further participation in the Games. It seems that Dr Goebbels tried to mediate between the Peruvian Ambassador and Olympic officials, but apparently without success. [41] Two days later, however, *The Times* reported:[42] *"The Peruvian Olympic team is not after all to make a premature departure from Berlin. The Peruvians have decided that to do so would be discourteous to their German hosts and the organisers of the Games, who, they agree, are not concerned with the trouble which arose out of the cancelling of the Peruvian football team's victory over Austria. A friendly football match is to be played between Germany and Peru.*

Hitler did not appear to be involved in these events at all, but excited crowds gathered in Lima, the Peruvian capital, and swirled about, first to the presidential Palace, where reference was made to a 'crafty Berlin decision', and then to the German Legation, which was stoned. [43] Dockers in Lima refused to load goods onto both German and Norwegian ships, presumably thinking that all northern Europeans were the same. A recent book, *Ese gol existe*, by the Peruvian author Luis Carlos Arias Schreiber, published in 2008, is reported to have *"produced an array of reports suggesting that the official version was accurate and criticised the Peruvian press which had been maligning the Nazis all these years."* [44]

40 Paul Doyle, "The forgotten story of ... football, farce and fascism at the 1936 Olympics," *The Guardian*, London, 24 November 2011.

41 "Discord at the Games," *The Times*, London, 12 August 1936.

42 "Peruvian Olympic Team to Stay in Berlin," *The Times*, London, 14 August 1936.

43 "German Legation in Lima Stoned, *The Times*, London, 12 August 1936.

44 Ibid.

LENI RIEFENSTAHL'S FILM

Germany's leading film-maker at the time, Leni Riefenstahl, made a widely acclaimed movie of the Olympics entitled, simply, *Olympia*, using a number of innovative techniques subsequently adopted by others. In its obituary, the BBC conceded that [45] *"Her Nazi documentaries were hailed as groundbreaking film-making, pioneering techniques involving cranes, tracking rails, and many cameras working at the same time."*

In her film, she gave much more coverage to Jesse Owens than to the American winner of the arduous decathlon, Glenn Morris, who was voted 'the greatest athlete in the world' by Olympic officials. Her fair-minded and brilliant portrayal of the Games, however, did not save her from boycott and persecution after WW2. [46]

---

45 "Film-maker Leni Riefenstahl dies," BBC News website, 9 September 2003.

46 Although she was never a member of the Nazi Party, Leni Riefenstahl was incarcerated from 1945 to 1948 in American and French concentration camps and prisons or under house arrest during the great post-War anti-Nazi witch-hunt. According to the BBC News website (9 September 2003), even in 2002, the year of her 100th birthday, she was "investigated for Holocaust denial,". However, she was never convicted of any offence – not even of any of the new retrospective 'crimes' created by the Allies.

Berlin school children assembled on the May Field for a display.

A triple American victory in the high jump

View from the tower of the Bell which "summoned the youth of the world."

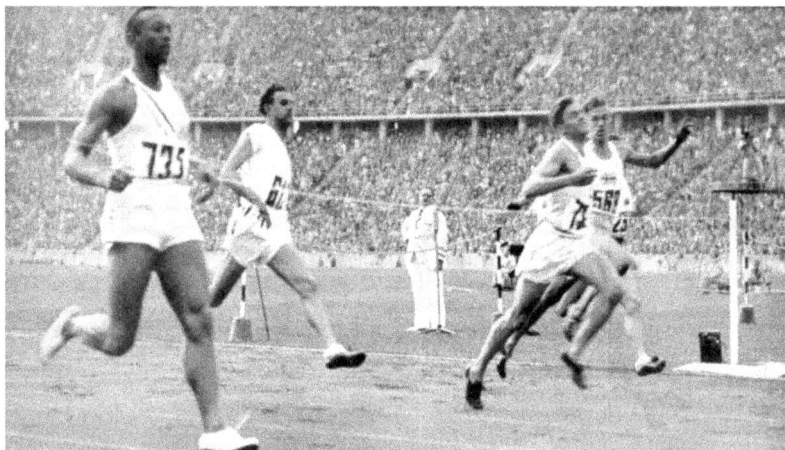

First semi-final. Owens did not extend himself but won in 10.4 seconds.

Ilona Elek-Schacherer (Hungary), Ellen Preis (Austria) and Helene Mayer (Germany)

HELENE MAYER

Having won the silver medal in fencing, Helene Meyer, who had a Jewish father, returned to the United States where she showed great strength of character in refusing to join in the anti-German chorus. She never spoke publicly against the Third Reich and has been quoted as saying: [47] *"Here in America the press denigrated the Olympics on purpose. It's all propaganda against Germany!! Didn't do them much good because . . . I have given a lot of speeches at clubs, universities and once even on the radio and I let them have it! Those windbags, who still cannot get over the fact that the Olympics in Berlin were the highlight of all the Olympics."* For several years, she displayed a photo of herself shaking hands with Hitler, who she apparently referred to as a *"cute little man."* She became good friends with Leni Riefenstahl and accompanied her on a US tour to promote her film on the Olympics. [48]

---

47 Carole Levy, "The Olympic Pause," *Jewish Magazine*, October High Holiday edition 2000. [Accessed from www.jewishmag.com, 25 October 2012.]

48 Ibid.

Telefunken camera for the German television network.

LIVE TELEVISION FIRST AT THE OLYMPICS

The first regular television service in the world was established in Germany in 1935. Further progress was demonstrated at the Berlin radio exhibition in 1936 and at the Berlin Olympic Games, where direct television cameras were first used, giving an immediate transmission of a scene. High-definition (by contemporary standards) television broadcasts of events, as they happened, were viewed in television halls on screens large enough to be watched by audiences of 300 people.[49]

This innovation led, of course, to current practice, when popular events can be watched on giant screens away from the crowded venues where they are taking place. This was one of many great technical and scientific developments in National Socialist Germany that are generally ignored or swept under the carpet today.

---

49 "Television in Berlin", Popular Wireless, 19th September 1936; "Television of Olympic Games", *The Times* [London], 18 July 1936.

WHO WON MOST MEDALS AT
THE BERLIN OLYMPICS 1936?

One book reviewer for a national British newspaper was to write, in 2001, of *"Germany, still smarting* [in 1942] *from defeats at the Berlin Olympics…"* [50]

A side heading for a note on the Olympics in a Time-Life book asserts that they provided *"A setback for Aryan Supremacy,"* [51] but it makes no mention of which country won the most medals or how many. The following table of leading medal winners at the 1936 Olympics can best show the extent of the defeats from which Germany was still supposedly smarting in 1942:

	Gold	Silver	Bronze	Points
Germany	33	26	30	181
United States	24	20	12	124
Italy	8	9	5	47
Finland	7	6	6	39
France	7	6	6	39
Hungary	10	1	5	37

50 Andy Martin, "Stalingrad with studs; Andy Martin hails the footballers who defied the Nazis." *Daily Telegraph*, 31 March 2001. The Daily Telegraph did not remind its readers that Britain had won only 14 medals (one more than Austria) in the same Games.

51 The New Order, part of *The Third Reich* series, Time-Life Books 1989, page 94.

Jesse Owens jumps 8.06 metres and sets an Olympic record.

THE JESSE OWENS SAGA

Although the Berlin Olympics has been acknowledged as the most massive sporting festival the world had yet seen, it is commonly remembered only because Jesse Owens and other African-American athletes supposedly humiliated and enraged the German Chancellor, causing him to snub them. A *Readers' Digest* reference book, for example, states:[52] *'In 1936, at the Berlin Olympics, Owens won four gold medals - for the 100m and 200m sprints, the sprint relay and the long jump. At the same time, as a black, he refuted the Nazi theory of Aryan supremacy. As a result, the German Chancellor, Adolf Hitler, who attended the Games, allegedly refused to acknowledge him, and left the stadium in a rage.'*

The facts, however, are that, on the first day of the Games[53] *"... Hitler was present to congratulate Hans Wolke, a German, for breaking the Olympian record for the shot put. He also congratulated three Finns who swept the 10,000-metre run as well as the German women who were placed first and second in the javelin throw. By the time the German entrants in the High Jump were eliminated it was dark and so he was not there to shake hands with the three American winners, two of who were black.*

---

52 The Reader's Digest *Illustrated Dictionary of Essential Knowledge* 1995, p 379.

53 Toland, pages 392-3.

This led the President of the International Olympian Committee to inform the Führer that, as guest of honour, he should henceforth congratulate all victors or none. Hitler chose the latter course and so did not meet Jesse Owens, who won four gold medals."

Hitler and his party left on a pre-arranged schedule. In any event, it may be noted that as, at the time he left the stadium, the High Jump competition had not yet been completed, he could not have known who would win. Hitler, as requested, did not invite any more winners to his box at the stadium. In view of his duties as Chancellor, which he took rather seriously, Hitler could hardly be expected to commit himself to be present for every event. Owens did not win his first medal until the following day. On his return to his native land Owens himself not only denied that Hitler had publicly turned his back on him, but claimed that Hitler did pay a tribute to him.

As one American newspaper reported [54] *"As for Adolf Hitler, Owens had nothing but kind words."* And it went on to quote Owens as follows: *"Hitler had a certain time to come to the stadium and a certain time to leave. It happened he had to leave before the victory ceremony after the 100 meters. But before he left I was on my way to a broadcast and passed near his box. He waved to me and I waved back. I think it bad taste to criticise the 'man of the hour' in another country."*

As Owens's biographer pointed out [55] "The yarn [that Hitler snubbed Owens], created by American sports writers, was repeated so often that people finally took it as fact"

---

54 "Owens arrives with kind words for all officials," United Press agency report, *The Pittsburg Press,* 24 August 1936.

55 William J Baker, *Jesse Owens: An American Life,* Macmillan, New York 1986, page 3.

GERMAN ATTITUDE TO OWENS

Owens was acclaimed by German spectators. His biographer noted [56] "German spectators also responded warmly to the young Owens ... Neither rain nor cold kept the crowd below 100,000 from the afternoon finals. They watched and applauded Jesse's every move. Unaccustomed to seeing black athletes, they were quickly won over by his dominant athleticism and friendly demeanour. In the Olympic Village, at the stadium, and on the streets of Berlin, they clamoured to touch him, to get his autograph, to snap his picture."

Evidently, the Germans took to Owens immediately.[57] *'German spectators gave him the warmest ovation of his life ...... after Jesse won his first heat, the entire stadium burst out in thunderous applause. From then on he received a loud ovation every time he walked onto the track.'*

All this was very much appreciated by Owens who, on his return home, talked at length about the Olympic Games, volunteering information without waiting for reporters to question him, saying [58] *"Germans were good sportsmen and their organisation of the games was faultless ... I was treated marvellous by everyone. Anything any of the American athletes, including myself, wanted they got for us."*

---

56 Ibid.

57 Baker, page 92.

58 "Owens arrives with kind words for all officials," United Press agency report, *The Pittsburg Press*, 24 August 1936.

RECOGNITION

In Germany, the Reemtsma tobacco company published a deluxe two-volume picture book to commemorate the Games.[59] It included seven pictures of Owens (more than any other athlete) and twelve pictures of black athletes in general. Hitler's picture appears only six times. Owens is hailed as 'the fastest man in the world'. One large picture in the book shows the chiselling of the victors' names in granite at the Olympic stadium, in particular showing the legend 'Owens U.S.A.' An article about the publication on the British Library website affirms that[60] "The reporting of the actual sporting events, which forms the bulk of the text, is generally even-handed. The achievements of Jesse Owens, acknowledged as 'the most popular man in the track and field events', and other black American athletes are fully recognised, as are the successes of Jewish medal winners (although without any reference, negative or positive, to their being Jewish).

---

59 Olympia 1936, Cigaretten-Bilderdienst Altona-Bahrenfeld", a subsidiary of the Reemtsma tobacco company, 1936.

60 "The Summer Olympics and Paralympics through the lens of social science," British Library, [www.bl.uk/sportandsociety - accessed 20 October 2012].

The Langemarck Hall memorial to the youths who fell in the War.

If, as is commonly believed, the Nazis strictly controlled everything published in Germany, the book must have been approved at a very high level.

Owens's name was, in fact, engraved three times on the Olympics Victors' stone of commemoration at the Berlin stadium. He won his fourth gold medal as part of the United States relay team, which was collectively honoured on the same plaque.

AMERICAN ATTITUDES TO OWENS

It is quite clear that the attitude of both the German government and German people to Owens was very positive. However, this was not so in the United States. Prior to the Olympics, Owens and other African-American athletes were not invited to the Sugar Bowl athletic meeting in New Orleans, but no one suggested that those games should be cancelled or boycotted.[61]

In the run-up to the 1936 Olympics, on the way to Butler Indoor Relays in Indianapolis,[62] *"... he* [Owens] *and his black friends were forbidden to enter a roadside café. They waited in the car for white team mates to bring them food, only to have the enraged owner of the café come out hollering that he didn't want 'to feed no nigger' on his premises."*

Owens and two other African-American athletes were also refused admission to a restaurant in Richmond, Indiana. [63] African-Americans in many parts of the United States had to stay in segregated hotels when travelling, whereas Owens was free to travel with and stay in the same hotels as whites in Germany. [64] On his return to the United States after the Olympics, Owens said: [65] *"After I came home from the 1936 Olympics with my four medals, it became increasingly apparent that everyone was going to slap me on the back, want to shake my hand or have me up to their suite. But no one was going to offer me a job.*

He was honoured with a traditional tickertape parade in New York, but [66]'when he arrived at the Waldorf Astoria hotel for a reception in his honour, he was instructed to take the service lift rather than the normal guest lift, which was reserved for whites.'

---

61 Baker, page 66.

62 Baker, page 67.

63 Ibid.

64 "Jesse Owens," Wikipedia. Accessed 30 July 2012.

65 Baker, page 150. Baker quoting here from I Have Changed, by Jesse Owens in collaboration with Paul Neimark 1972.

66 Broughton, op.cit.

A German officer tries his linguistic skills on two Philippine athletes.

Despite his great success in Berlin Owens found life hard when he returned home. He was deprived of a career when expelled from the American Amateur Athletics Union because he had put a chance to profit from his fame before a foreign tour. Reduced to *"becoming a kind of circus act to support his family,"* he would run against cars, motorbikes, dogs and horses. He had jobs as a janitor and petrol pump attendant and remarked that 'you can't eat four gold medals'. Three years after his Olympic triumphs he was bankrupted.[67] Subsequently he devoted much of his life to under-privileged youth and became an inspirational speaker and public relations consultant.

When 52 years old he was fined $3,000 dollars for Federal income tax evasion for not keeping up with his tax returns. The maximum penalty was four years jail, but the judge seemed sympathetic, spending over half an hour reviewing the work that he had done in youth counselling. "You have been subjected to pressure of public appearances," the judge said, "You have been too generous."[68]

---

67 Ibid.

68 "Tax evasion costs Owens $3,000," Pittsburgh Post-Gazette, 2 February 1966.

F.D. Roosevelt won a landslide election victory in 1936, but he refused to meet Jesse Owens for fear of upsetting white voters.

ROOSEVELT'S SNUB

President Franklin D Roosevelt never congratulated Owens or invited him [or any of the other African-American athletes] to the White House after the Berlin Olympics. Owens said [69] *"Hitler didn't snub me – it was FDR who snubbed me."*

It has been suggested that[70] *"If President Roosevelt ever considered such a gesture in 1936, he quickly dismissed it from his mind. His posing for a picture besides Jesse Owens, Ralph Metcalfe, Cornelius Johnson, and all the other black medallists would have lost rather than gained him votes in the South."* In stark contrast, Hitler is reported to have sent Jesse a commemorative inscribed cabinet photograph of himself.[71]

Like most successful politicians Roosevelt put votes before principles, but he would probably not have invited the African-American athletes to the White House anyway. For, even in the Second World War, when he was politically unassailable, he sanctified the segregation of African-Americans into separate units in the army. Interestingly, it seems that Blacks were not segregated in the German armed forces, or in the Hitler Youth though, of course, there were far fewer Blacks in Germany than in the United States.

---

69 Broughton, op cit.

70 Baker, page 147.

71 "Owens Weighs His Pro Offers," *The Baltimore Sun*, 18 August 1936.

OWENS ON HITLER

Jesse returned to the United States in the prestigious liner the *Queen Mary*. His biographer records that [72] *"By the time the Queen Mary docked, Jesse had gained his composure. He masterfully handled a barrage of questions from reporters. Everything now seemed 'fine'. 'Hitler?' 'Why, he was fine ... ... Stories about him refusing to cheer the Americans are not true at all'."*

During subsequent campaigning by Jesse for the Republicans in the Presidential election,[73] *"Large crowds turned out to hear him and to get his autograph afterwards. Mostly they heard a series of anecdotes about the Berlin Olympics - that the Germans were wonderfully efficient, that Hitler was 'a man of dignity'."*

It is reported that Jesse, himself the grandson of slaves, was *"impatient with American claims of moral superiority over the Nazis."* He is quoted as saying [74] *"After all those stories about Hitler and his snub, I came back to my native country and I couldn't ride in the front of a bus, I had to go to the back door. I couldn't live where I wanted. Now what's the difference?"* One difference, perhaps, was that Jews in Germany were not forced to sit in the back of buses!

---

72 Baker, page 124.

73 Ibid, page 137.

74 Ibid.

Olympic structures in the modern style. The circular passageway of the Berlin
Olympic Stadium, a masterpiece of the architect, Werner March.

The exterior of the Stadium was coated with limestone.

THE BERGMANN CONTROVERSY

Gretel Bergmann, who achieved a German record in the women's high jump of 1.51 metres in 1931, came to England in 1933 after she had been expelled by her club for being Jewish. In 1934 she won the high jump in the British Championships but then accepted an invitation to return to Germany and take part in pre-Olympic training as part of the German team from 1934 to 1936.

It is claimed that her return was prompted by concern for her parents, who were still resident in Germany. However, Arnd Krüger, the sports academician, has stated that when he interviewed her for NDR2-Radio (Hamburg) (aired November 9, 1988), she pointed out that she had returned from Britain to compete for Germany as she had not received a British passport and could, therefore, not compete for Britain.[75] On returning to Germany she was invited by the Schild organisation to train at their centre in Stuttgart. According to one report, in 1935 she became the only Jewish athlete at a Stuttgart sports school, but was still treated as an equal by her classmates.[76]

---

75 Arnd Krüger, "German Jewish Sport 1898-1938 and the Anti-Semitic Discourse," *Journal of Sport History*, Volume 26,Number 2, Summer 1999, Note 36, page 37. Krüger, professor of sports studies at Göttingen University, headed his article with an alleged Brownshirt slogan, "Once the Olympics are through, we'll beat up the Jew," but he gave as his source for this slogan a paper produced by German exiles in Paris in 1936.

76 "German Jewish athletes prepare for the track and field Olympics," US Holocaust

BERGMANN LEFT OUT OF FINAL TEAM

When the final selection for participation in the Games had been made, Bergmann received a letter notifying her that her recent performances were not good enough and she was left out of the team, but given free tickets to watch the Games. It should be noted that six months before the Games, The Times, in reporting that Mayer had arrived in Germany for training and preliminary trials, noted that Bergmann might win citizenship of the Reich if she qualified for the Olympic team, adding [77] *"but meanwhile she is not regarded as being in the first three."*

It is widely alleged that she was left out because she was Jewish and Hitler did not want a Jewess to get a gold medal.[78] This author has found no irrefutable evidence that the German officials were not acting in good faith. There seems to have been no attempt to prevent Bergmann from taking part in – and winning - the Women's High Jump at the Wurtemberg Regional Championships in Germany in 1936[79]. Also, Mayer was selected for the Olympics and won a silver medal and she may well have won a gold – as she had at a previous Olympics, though Mayer was only half-Jewish.

Germany's detractors point out that Bergmann was not told of her omission from the team until after the American athletes had set sail for the Games, so it would be too late for them to change their minds about participating. Of course, it would have been possible for the Americans to sail back in disgust if they had so wished. Also it might be noted that no athlete from any other country, including Germany's neighbours, seemed to have changed their minds about competing, though it would have been easy for them to do so – and be generously acclaimed for doing so.

Memorial Museum [ushmm.org/photoarchives – accessed 29 October 2012].

77 "German Olympic Fencing Team: Jewess may be picked," *The Times*, London, 19 February 1936.

78 For example, a plaque on a house in Berlin-Wilmersdorf (where a sports complex was named after Bergmann) states that "... Because of her Jewish origins, the Nazis prevented her from taking part in the 1936 Olympics."

79 Some accounts say this was 1935.

It is also pointed out that, less than three weeks before the letter notifying her non-selection, Bergmann had equalled the German record (held by Elfried Kaun) of 1.60 metres for the women's high jump.[80] Sometimes it is said that her record jump of 1.60 metres would have ensured her a medal. However, even assuming she could repeat the performance, it would not have guaranteed a medal as all three actual medal winners cleared that height at the Games and their placings had to be settled by a 'jump-off'. So Bergmann would only have been one of four competitors on 1.60 metres.

Bergmann may have been unfairly treated, but it seems a little odd that, for example, Britain's two most authoritative newspapers, *The Times* and the *Manchester Guardian*, and the *New York Times* did not even mention the controversy at the time, let alone seek details of the late pre-Olympic performances that dissatisfied the German team officials. It may be that the officials were pressed on the matter at the time and asked for details by someone, but this author has not found any reference to any such approach. Whatever the real reason for her non-selection, it seems clear that the responsible officials saw no need to take account of, or appease, international opinion. If she was unfairly treated, of course, it would bring justifiable discredit on the people responsible but it would have been out of keeping with the sportsmanlike way in which the Games were generally organised.

BERGMANN AND PARENTS EMIGRATE

Bergmann immigrated to the United States with her fiancé in 1937. In 1940 transport to England was arranged for the rest of her family, who finally immigrated to America after being interned in Britain as 'enemy aliens'. [81]No harm seems to have come to Bergman or her parents and there did not seem to be any restrictions on them leaving Germany if they had wished, even after the war had started.

---

80 Some accounts say that this record was achieved on 30 June 1936, but the house plaque (see note 79) states 27 June.

81 See note 77

THE RATJEN CONTROVERSY

The controversy took another turn when, two years later, it was discovered, by the German authorities, that Dora Ratjen was really a man. This has given rise to claims that Ratjen was brought into the team to replace Bergmann.[82] Sometimes it is claimed that the Nazis knew Ratjen was a man and brought her in the team to win a medal unfairly.

One thing is certain: Ratjen could not have been a replacement for Bergmann as the Germans were entitled to enter three competitors in the high jump, but they only entered two. In other words Bergman could have taken part in addition to Kaun and Ratjen. It may be noted also that the Germans withheld their right to enter a maximum number of competitors in the 50 kilometre walk – where there seemed to be no question of omissions on racial grounds.

Ratjen was born with improperly formed genitalia that led the midwife at birth to wrongly determine him to be a girl. Although it seems his parents had some doubts they brought him up as a girl, dressed him in girls' clothes and he grew up trapped in a wrong gender world among girls. He was a loner, avoiding

82 See note 77

Dora Ratjen represented Germany in the 1936 Olympics.

parties, but became interested in sport, joined an athletics club and excelled in the high jump, eventually finding himself chosen for pre-Olympic training in the German team for the 1936 games. It was here that he met Elfried Kaun and Gretel Bergmann for the first time, and photos showed 'the three women in cheerful relaxed mood.' [83] Bergmann is quoted as saying: [84] *"I never had any suspicions, not even once. In the communal shower we wondered why she never showed herself naked. It was grotesque that someone could still be that shy at the age of 17. We just thought, 'She's strange. She's odd'."*

Though Kaun thought Ratjen was very masculine, she never dreamt that her fellow athlete was a man. As she remembered:[85] *"We had a very good relationship in the training camps, on trips, and during competitions. But no-one knew or noticed anything about her different sexuality."* It seems clear, therefore, that Ratjen fooled everyone.

---

83 Stefan Berg, "How Dora the Man Competed in the Woman's High Jump," Der Spiegel online, 15 September 2009. [accessed 18 October 2012]

84 Ibid.

85 Ibid.

EXPOSURE

Two years after the Olympics Ratjen, still successfully posing as a woman, won the gold medal in the high jump competition at the European championships, setting a new world record. A few days later, in September 1938, the police arrested him after the conductor on a train reported a man posing as a woman. He was examined by a physician, who confirmed that he was a man. Criminal proceedings began on the suspicion of fraud and Ratjen was sent to a sports sanatorium for further examinations, which confirmed that she was a he. In January 1939 his entry at the birth registry was amended to record his true sex and he changed his forename to Heinrich. A few weeks later the criminal proceedings were shelved, on the grounds that the deception was not carried out for monetary gain. Ratjen had already admitted he was a man on his arrest and he promised to cease engaging in sport with immediate effect. His victory at the European championships was expunged from the record and he returned the gold medal, which was later presented to the runner-up.[86]

Steps were taken to rehabilitate Ratjen into normal life. The last note on the police files, in August 1939, states that he was given a work book, invalidity papers, and membership of the German Labour Front; the amalgamated trade union. He was issued with new ID and work papers and taken to Hanover 'as a working man', according to the document. The note was sent to the Reich Sports Ministry, various police stations, and the relevant courts. There is nothing to suggest that senior civil servants tried to keep the case a secret or restrict the number of people who were aware of it. [87]

It seems that the German authorities dealt with the matter with some understanding and sympathy. No one was prosecuted and everything was done to give Ratjen a new start. In normal circumstances the young man (he was still only 19 years old) would have left the past behind him and enjoyed a new life, liberated from any need to deceive. But it was not to be.

---

86 Ibid.

87 Ibid.

EXPLOITATION

After the war Ratjen took over his parents' bar in Bremen and resisted numerous attempts to interview him, but the American news magazine *Time* published an article in 1966 about female impostors in which Ratjen was featured. Presumably the magazine had managed to interview him as it reported that he *"tearfully confessed"* that the Nazis had forced him to represent Germany as a woman. It also quoted him as saying, "For three years I lived the life of a girl. It was most dull.' [88]

Shortly after the *Time* article an item on the same subject appeared in *Life* magazine, which informed its readers that, after World War II, Ratjen[89] *"Admitted having been an out-and-out fake – forced to compete by the Hitler Youth Movement to win medals for the Third Reich."*

Ratjen's exposure as a female impostor is continually raked up by the anti-Nazi industry and a film entitled *Berlin 1936* was produced to dramatise the story, although Ratjen was portrayed under a different name. The film was not actually shown in public before 2009, the year after Ratjen's death, though it may well have been conceived and worked on before his death. It was given the air of authenticity by the inclusion of an interview with the real Gretel Bergmann at the end. The film created a new flurry of interest in Ratjen.

The story as told by *Time* and *Berlin 1936* was refuted by *Der Spiegel*, a highly respected international news magazine, in 2009. It pointed out that the information about Ratjen in the *Time* article was meagre and imprecise, referring to him as 'Hermann' and claiming that he was working as a waiter in Bremen. *"Unfortunately,"* says Der Spiegel, *" this portrayal was the one that was circulated from that moment on, and repeated else-where in the press."*[90]

88 "Track & Field: Preserving the difference," Time, 16 September 1966.

89 "Sex inspections for female contestants stir international furore," Life, 7 October 1966.

90 Stefan Berg, op cit.

Der Spiegel also made public a file containing the findings of an investigation conducted in 1938 and 1939. This was provided by the Department for Sexual Medicine at Kiel University Hospital, whose head, Professor Hartmut Bosinski, had been researching the case because it showed that boys can't be brought up to be girls.[91]

The previously unknown police file contains statement by Ratjen, his father and many others. It shows that Dora attended a girls' school and was religiously confirmed in 1932 as a girl. Ratjen told the police in 1938: [92] *"My parents brought me up as a girl. I therefore wore girl's clothes all my childhood. But from the age of 10 or 11 I started to realize I wasn't female, but male. However I never asked my parents why I had to wear women's clothes even though I was male."*

According to *Der Spiegel*, the file[93] *"contains not the slightest shred of evidence of the alleged plot. In fact, the documents suggest the Nazis only discovered the true identity of their model athlete much later."* Even a five-page report personally signed by security chief Reinhard Heydrich *"contains no evidence of any previous manipulation."*

It seems clear that there was no Nazi plot. Further, it would surely have been easy for the Nazis, especially in view of their reputation for utter ruthlessness, to effect a cover-up as soon as the deception was discovered, but they came clean straight away, ensuring that the previous high jump record was restored and returned the gold medal to the organisers of the European Championships so it could be presented to the runner-up – who happened to be the Hungarian Jewess Ibolya Csàk.

Other commentators on the Berlin 1936 story do not appear to be as diligent as Der Spiegel. Some even got Ratjen's forename wrong, calling him Horst or Hermann instead of Heinrich.

---

91 Ibid.

92 Ibid.

93 Ibid.

A small spectator from China with his mother in the Stadium.

This may, perhaps, indicate how little they cared for Ratjen the person. The BBC (British Broadcasting Corporation) news website stated that [94] *"Dora Ratjen - whose real name was Horst Ratjen - continued to compete in the high jump for another two years."*

At the time of the Games, of course, Ratjen's real name was Dora, and remained so until his name change – to Heinrich – in 1939. It may be that the BBC was getting him mixed up with the rather more famous Horst Wessel.

For the international media, Ratjen's story had everything: salaciousness, humiliation, embarrassment, disappointment - and a stick to beat the Nazis with. Unfortunately, it seems to come apart when faced with the facts.

---

94 "The Jewish Jumper and the Male Impostor ", BBC News, 9 September 2009.

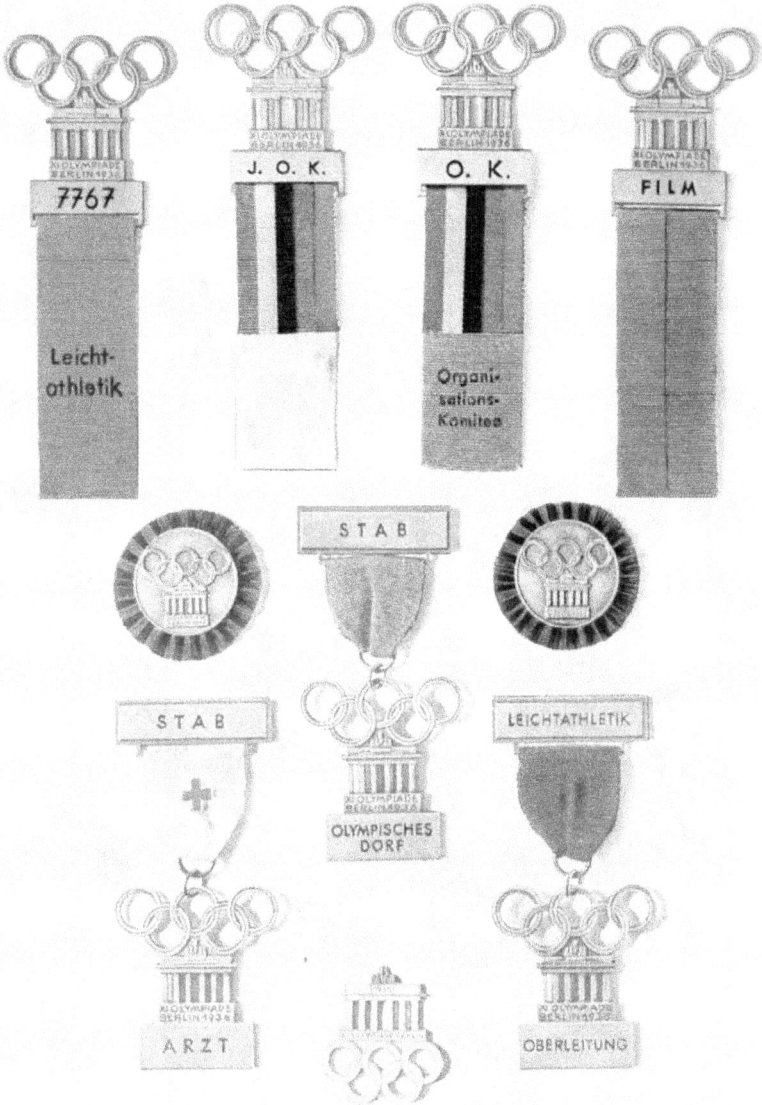

Examples of the Olympic badges for athletes and officials. Designs by Prof. Walter Raemisch. The small badges with rosettes were worn by the members of the International Physical Education Students' Encampment (green) and the International Youth Encampment (blue). The visitor's badge, which was sold publicly is depicted at the lower centre.

"This Europe of ours is too small for a war, but it is large enough to contain a field of combat upon which the youth of the world will win a decisive battle for the cause of peace. To cooperate in the solution of this task is the sincere and sacred wish of the entire German nation." - The Reich War Minister, Field Marshal von Blomberg

The gold chain designed by Walter E. Lemcke, Berlin for the members of the International Olympic Committee.

The Eleventh Olympic Games occupied the limelight of international publicity in 1936. Germany was assigned the honourable task of presenting this largest sporting festival that the world has ever seen. German organization, German hospitality and German enthusiasm for the Olympic ideals created the background for an incomparable example of true Olympic competition. The German nation thus provided the world with renewed proof of its capability and its willingness to cooperate in large international projects designed to further universal peace.

Dr. Goebbels

Evening entertainment in the main auditorium of the Hindenburg House.

The Government reception in the State Opera House. In the centre loge, the royal guests from Bulgaria and Sweden, and Frau Göring seated; General Göring standing.

Traffic arrangements at the Brandenburg Gate, Berlin.

The ceremony to welcome the arrival of the Olympic
torch at Königsufer in Dresden.

THE CLOSING CEREMONY

After "a fortnight of unprecedented spectacles, crowds and athletic achievement," an "insatiable enthusiasm" was still evident at the closing ceremony according the special correspondent of Britain's leading newspaper. Count Baillet-Latour offered the gratitude of the International Olympic Committee to Chancellor Hitler, the German people, the Berlin authorities and the organisers of the Games. His final words were:[95] *"May the Olympic torch be carried throughout the ages with ever greater eagerness, courage, and honour for the good of humanity."*

The style, pageantry, enthusiasm and international friendship of the Berlin Olympics undoubtedly set the tone for the great spectacles that the world witnesses today every four years although, unfortunately, they have now become blighted by unashamed and aggressive commercialism.

---

95 "End of Berlin Games," *The Times*, London, 17 August 1936.

www.ingramcontent.com/pod-product-compliance
Lightning Source LLC
Chambersburg PA
CBHW070258290326
41930CB00041B/2638